JOS

FROM BONDAGE TO BREAKTHROUGH

EXPERIENCE HEALING, WHOLENESS, AND VICTORY THROUGH THE ANOINTING OIL

From Bondage to Breakthrough: Experience Healing, Wholeness, and Victory through the Anointing Oil
Copyright © 2017
Joseph Prince Ministries
P.O. Box 2115
Fort Mill, SC 29716
USA

Printed in the United States of America
First edition, first print: December 2017

INTRODUCTION

Thank you for requesting this booklet. What you hold in your hand is a faith-building resource that will help you experience a greater measure of God's blessings as you learn exciting truths about the anointing oil.

These are truths that God has given me during my time of study on the topic and I hope they will open your eyes to see the benefits and power of Jesus' finished work embodied in the anointing oil.

My purpose for writing this booklet is two-fold: To introduce you to the anointing oil as it relates to healing and seeing the manifold blessings of God released in your life. And, to answer questions you may have about the anointing oil. If you are not familiar with its use, you will learn its significance to you as a believer, why it is God's ordained channel to deliver you from every bondage, and when and how you can use the oil to release victory in your very area of challenge.

If you are familiar with or have already been using the anointing oil, I believe this practical guide will help you walk in a greater measure of health, protection, and freedom from every bondage as you apply the anointing oil with fresh revelation and faith.

You'll also find a section featuring real-life stories of precious people who received freedom from chronic conditions and who were protected from very real threats as they applied the anointing oil and put their trust in the Lord. May these praise reports inspire you to know how much God wants to do the same for you today!

Beloved, I pray that as you take time to read and meditate on the Scriptures, truths, and testimonies in this booklet, you will find your life overflowing with our Lord Jesus' health, supply, and victory!

Grace always,

Joseph Prince

WHAT IS THE SIGNIFICANCE

OF THE ANOINTING OIL FOR BELIEVERS?

The
anointing oil
is a divine channel
by which
all believers
can walk in
divine healing,
protection,
and increase
and wholeness
in every area
of life.

And He will love you and bless you and multiply you; He will also bless the fruit of your womb and the fruit of your land, **your grain and your new wine and your oil**, the increase of your cattle and the offspring of your flock, in the land of which He swore to your fathers to give you. You shall be blessed above all peoples; there shall not be a male or female barren among you or among your livestock. And the Lᴏʀᴅ will take away from you all sickness, and will afflict you with none of the terrible diseases of Egypt which you have known, but will lay *them* on all those who hate you.

DEUTERONOMY 7:13–15 (BOLDFACE MINE)

The anointing oil, together with the Holy Communion, are God's divine channels by which all believers can walk in His divine healing, protection from diseases and other evils, and increase and wholeness in every area of life. In the first verse of the above Scripture, we see how these three elements—the grain and the wine (representing the Holy Communion), and the oil (representing the anointing oil)—are specifically mentioned by the Lord, and part and parcel of His loving you and multiplying His blessing in your life.

God is telling us that because He loves us, His beloved children, He wants to bless and multiply us. Notice that we will see ourselves "blessed above all peoples" after He first blesses our grain, our new wine, and our oil.

Why is that so?

It's because all these elements speak of His Son and His finished work at the cross. God is saying that when we take time to meditate on and declare how Jesus at the cross has paid for our wholeness in every area through our partaking of the Holy Communion and application of the anointing oil, His victory over sin, sickness, oppression, and lack is released in our lives.

Beloved, today, when you bring the oil to God and apply it with the revelation of how our Lord Jesus has purchased by His shed blood every blessing you need, you are declaring your faith in Jesus and His finished work alone. You are remembering how He was crushed so that you can have the fresh oil of His healing, His favor, and His supply in your body, your family, your career, and your ministry. And when you do this, you will see His practical blessings flow into your area of need.

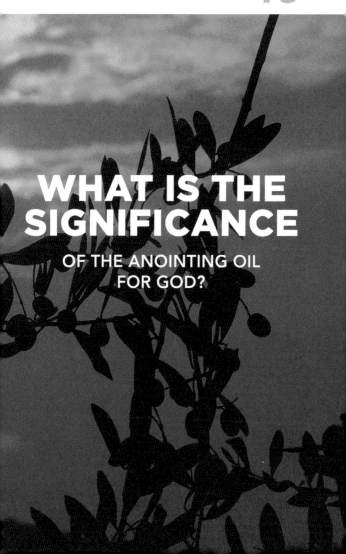

WHAT IS THE SIGNIFICANCE

OF THE ANOINTING OIL
FOR GOD?

Made from
the finest
olive fruits,
the anointing
oil is a picture
of Jesus'
finished work
on the cross.

Made from the finest olive fruits, the anointing oil is a picture of Jesus' finished work on the cross. Just as bread and wine are made through a process of crushing, olive oil can only be obtained by crushing the olive fruit. All these speak of the crushing of Jesus to become the bread of life for us at the cross:

But he was pierced for our transgressions, he was crushed for our iniquities; the punishment that brought us peace was on him, and by his wounds we are healed.

ISAIAH 53:5 NIV

Beloved, Jesus came to be crushed, to be bruised, to be scourged, and to be pierced. This is so that all that He is and all that He has—His health, peace, abundance, favor, wholeness, and life—will flow out into your life.

To extract the oil, both the olive fruit and its seed have to be crushed by a great weight in an olive press. In the same manner, Jesus was crushed under the burden and weight of our sins and under the judgment of a holy God. He was crushed like the olive fruit to become the anointing oil that blesses, heals, and protects us today.

Did you know that in biblical times, the small olive fruit had to be crushed a number of times before all its oil was extracted?

Sometime ago when I was in Capernaum, the hometown of Jesus, I visited an olive press. The Israeli guide explained that olive fruits were put in the press and crushed three times with a huge millstone.

The first press produced extra virgin olive oil, which was used to light the Jewish temple. The oil from the second press was used for medicine, while the oil from the third or last press was used for making soap.

The Holy Spirit revealed to me that each of these pressings spoke of what our Lord went through for us at the cross, right down even to the order of their occurrence! Jesus was also pressed three times.

Beginning in Gethsemane, which means "oil press," our Lord experienced the first press causing Him to sweat great drops of blood (see Luke 22:44). There, Jesus dealt with the power of darkness so that we can be called "out of darkness into His marvelous light" and walk continuously in this light (see Luke 22:53, 1 Pet. 2:9). Today, His light also gives us spiritual discernment and wisdom in our everyday concerns.

The second press (for medicine) took place after Jesus was brought from Gethsemane and scourged. His body was so violently and ruthlessly lashed by the Roman whips that His bones were exposed—all to buy us healing, health, and wholeness for our bodies.

Jesus is our "medicine" because "by His stripes we are healed" (Isa. 53:5).

The last press (for the making of soap for cleansing) happened at the cross. Jesus was crushed under the fiery indignation of a holy and righteous God because He was carrying our sins and was being punished for them. His blood was shed at Calvary to wash away all our sins, making us as white as snow (see Isa. 1:18).

Beloved, bringing the oil to God and applying it biblically is to reflect on the three presses that Jesus went through for you. It is considering how like the olive fruit, our Lord was thoroughly crushed so that you can be delivered from the powers of darkness that attempt to crush you with curses of sickness, mental oppression, and premature death. Realize that He went through all that suffering only because He loves you and wants you to enjoy the fullness of all the benefits He has obtained for you as you use the oil!

WHEN CAN I USE

THE ANOINTING OIL?

Apply
the anointing
oil to express
your faith
in Jesus'
finished work
to bring
about the
breakthroughs
you need.

WHEN YOU NEED HEALING

If there's pain in your body, if you have been suffering from a chronic illness or long-term condition, I encourage you to use the anointing oil to experience your healing breakthrough. Is this biblical? Absolutely. The Gospel of Mark describes how Jesus' disciples anointed the sick with oil and healed them:

> **So they went out and preached that *people* should repent. And they cast out many demons, and anointed with oil many who were sick, and healed *them*.**
>
> MARK 6:12–13

In the New Testament, we also see the early church using the anointing oil to bring healing to the afflicted. James 5:14–15 tells us that when the elders of the church visited the sick, they anointed the sick person with oil in the name of the Lord.

> **Is anyone among you sick? Let him call for the elders of the church, and let them pray over him, anointing him with oil in the name of the Lord. And the prayer of**

faith will save the sick, and the Lord will raise him up. And if he has committed sins, he will be forgiven.

These verses clearly show us that using the anointing oil on the sick is not a superstition, but an expression of faith to release God's divine healing power.

Today, if you have a sickness, you can anoint your head or the afflicted part of your body with anointing oil and say, "Father, I thank You that by Jesus' stripes, I am healed. Jesus was crushed for my wholeness. Therefore, I command this sickness to leave me in Jesus' name."

You can also anoint and pray for the healing of your loved ones in faith using the anointing oil. A lady who follows my ministry heard about the benefits of using the anointing oil through my teaching and applied it on her daughter who was suffering from severe eczema on both her heels.

The pain brought on by the condition was so intense that there were days her daughter could only walk on her toes. The lady took hold of a small bottle of olive oil and prayed over it. And where three years of using prescribed creams did nothing to alleviate the condition, the eczema cleared up after three weeks of applying the anointing oil to her daughter's feet and declaring by faith that by Jesus' stripes, she was healed! The girl has never walked with any discomfort since. All glory to God!

Beloved, when the anointing oil is used with a revelation of Jesus' finished work, healing manifests! Sometimes the healing is immediate. Sometimes it takes longer. But if you're dealing with symptoms in your body, keep using the oil in faith knowing it is but a matter of time before the healing that Jesus accomplished for you comes to pass in your body!

WHEN YOU NEED FREEDOM FROM ANY OPPRESSION OR BONDAGE

In the Old Testament, the anointing oil was a symbol of the Holy Spirit and was used mainly for consecration and sanctification by the prophets and kings. But that's not all. Isaiah 10:27 tells us the anointing oil was used to break bondages by destroying every yoke of the enemy:

**It shall come to pass in that day *that*
his burden will be taken away from your
shoulder, and his yoke from your neck,
and the yoke will be destroyed because
of the anointing oil.**

What is this verse saying and what exactly is this yoke?

The word "his" in the verse refers to the Assyrians, Israel's enemies back then. Today, it represents the enemy who seeks to oppress you with burdens that weigh you down, like stress, worries, anxieties, and strife.

The "yoke" speaks of subjugation or oppression, the way an ox is made to bear a yoke that forces it to pull a cart and move in a certain direction. Addiction, for example, is a yoke that the enemy uses to drag you under and keep you where he wants you—defeated and unable to live the abundant life.

Beloved, if this feels familiar, know that you don't have to stay under the devil's oppression. You don't have to stay bound. You can see the chains of your addiction—whether to pills, drugs, alcohol, food, or depressive thoughts—destroyed when you start using the anointing oil.

When you use the anointing oil conscious of how Christ was crushed to give you victory over the addiction that is controlling your life, you release the power of the Holy Spirit in you to destroy that bondage! Apply the anointing oil and be set free!

WHEN YOU WANT TO RELEASE THE FAVOR, GOOD SUCCESS, OR PROTECTION OF GOD

Besides breaking bondages and for healing, you can also use the anointing oil for protection. For example, you can anoint your children with oil as you pray the Lord's protection, favor, wisdom, and right-place-right-time blessing over them before they go to bed every night or before they go to school.

Or if you have a shop or business that doesn't seem to be doing well, you can anoint your shop or office with oil and declare, "I call my business favored and flourishing with success in Jesus' name."

Perhaps you have difficulty sleeping at night. Well, you can anoint your pillow with oil and say, "Jesus gives me, His beloved, sweet sleep."

Maybe you have to give a sales presentation or counsel someone. Before you do so, you can anoint your lips with oil, asking God for wisdom and for Him to speak through you.

What is important to know here is that the anointing oil is not some kind of magic potion. Neither is it a superstition or formula for quick success. To apply the anointing oil is to tangibly express your faith in Jesus' finished work to bring about the breakthroughs and miracles you need. And to help you see how others have used the anointing oil and experienced their breakthroughs, I've included a few real-life testimonies of precious people at the end of this booklet to encourage you.

HOW DO I
GET STARTED

WITH THE ANOINTING OIL?

When
you pray over
the oil in
Jesus' name,
God sets it
apart and it
becomes holy
anointing oil.

Now that you know what the anointing oil symbolizes and how it can bless you, you might be wondering, "How do I get hold of the anointing oil?"

It is simple. Just get olive oil and pray over it. We recommend using olive oil but you can use other types of oil if you like. Just remember that you may be applying it on your skin, so use oils you are comfortable with.

You can bring the bottle of oil to church and have a pastor or leader pray over it, or you can pray over it yourself. Understand that on its own, your bottle of oil has no supernatural power. But when you pray over it in Jesus' name, God sets it apart and it becomes holy anointing oil. It is the anointing of God on the oil (because it always pleases God to be reminded of His Son's finished work) and the expression of faith when you use the oil that release His blessings.

Here is a simple prayer you can use. Hold the bottle of oil in your hands and say:

Father in heaven, in and of itself, this bottle of oil is just oil. But I ask You, Father, in the name of the Lord Jesus Christ, anoint this oil I hold in my hands. Anoint it and set it apart for Your holy purposes. Make it holy anointing oil.

Use it for Your glory, Father. Use it to make those on whom it is applied healthy, strong, and youthful, with sickness and disease far from them.

Father, I pray that as it is set apart right now for holy and consecrated purposes, may this oil bring down Your glory, bring down Your miracles. Wherever it is applied, may it turn darkness into light. May it turn lack into abundance. May it turn sickness into healing. May there be wonderful restoration, provision, and fruitfulness. May there even be the raising of the dead.

Father, I thank You that this bottle of oil is now holy anointing oil. In the name of Jesus I pray, Amen.

Now, the bottle of oil you have just prayed over is no longer natural oil. It is holy anointing oil. It is anointed with the power of God to release blessings into your life, blessings that Jesus suffered and died to give you. Start using it for God's glory!

HOW IMPORTANT IS IT

TO HAVE THE GRAIN, THE WINE, AND THE OIL IN OUR LIVES?

To walk
in a greater
measure of
His healing
and blessings,
God wants you
to always
have the
grain, wine,
and oil
in your life.

To walk in a greater measure of His healing and blessings, God wants you to always have the grain, wine, and oil in your life. Notice how they are often mentioned together in the context of God's blessings to His people:

And He will love you and bless you and multiply you; He will also bless the fruit of your womb and the fruit of your land, your grain and your new wine and your oil, the increase of your cattle and the offspring of your flock, in the land of which He swore to your fathers to give you.

DEUTERONOMY 7:13

"Then I will give *you* the rain for your land in its season, the early rain and the latter rain, that you may gather in your grain, your new wine, and your oil."

DEUTERONOMY 11:14

Hezekiah had very great riches and honor. And he made himself treasuries for silver, for gold, for precious stones, for spices, for shields, and for all kinds of desirable items;

storehouses for the harvest of grain, wine, and oil; and stalls for all kinds of livestock, and folds for flocks.

2 CHRONICLES 32:27–28

In the New Testament, when Jesus instituted the Holy Communion—the grain and the wine—we find the oil there too because He would soon be pressed like an olive fruit in the garden of Gethsemane (which means "oil press" in Hebrew).

Beloved, there are no insignificant details in the Bible. God put these three items together because He wants us to always remember the finished work of our Lord Jesus at the cross, as well as the benefits that He has wrought for us believers through His sacrifice.

The grain and the wine of the Holy Communion speak of our Lord's broken body and shed blood, and the oil represents the anointing oil. And when you partake of the Holy Communion in faith, and apply the anointing oil by faith, you are appropriating the benefits of the Lord's sacrifice for yourself by faith.

In essence, you are saying, "Lord, You did this for me. You went to the cross and Your sacrifice avails much for me. I receive all that You suffered and died for me to enjoy, such as health, healing, wholeness for my body, spirit, and mind, provision, protection, and so much more!"

• • •

PRAISE
REPORTS

Healed of Chronic Pain in Right Shoulder

NOEL | AUSTRALIA

I suffered from chronic pain in my right shoulder for about twelve months. Medical investigations showed that I had osteoarthritis and bone spurring due to joint damage.

The pain persisted despite physiotherapy and medication. When I visited the doctor for corticosteroid injections, he suggested undergoing an MRI, suspecting a torn rotator cuff. I chose not to have the MRI but continued on a synthetic morphine drug twice a day, paracetamol four times a day, along with an anti-inflammatory drug. However, the pain persisted, and was especially excruciating in the mornings.

Thankfully, through Pastor Prince's teachings, I learned to partake of the Holy Communion for my healing. An elder also anointed me with oil as he prayed for my shoulder.

About two weeks ago, I woke up with NO pain and found that I could move my shoulder freely and without discomfort! I have since remained pain-free and have no need for medication anymore. PRAISE GOD! Thank you, Pastor Prince, for faithfully preaching the gospel of grace!

Life Transformed, No Longer Depressed and Suicidal

SARA | NEVEDA, UNITED STATES

I used to dabble in witchcraft and terrorize my family with my anger issues. I felt bleak about my life and would cut myself. I didn't believe in God and thought Christianity was a joke. I also attempted suicide more than once as I thought I wasn't worth anything to anyone.

But I started watching and listening to some Christian programs upon my mother's encouragement. I stopped feeling suicidal but nothing else changed. Then, I tried New Age practices to "fix" myself—I'd smoke cigarettes while visualizing myself happy. That also did not work.

While getting ready for bed one night, I started having thoughts of killing myself again. When I refused those thoughts, I heard negative voices in my head telling me, "You're worthless, ugly, no one loves you. You're killing your mother being the way you are. Everyone hates you. You don't deserve to live."

That's when I began having horrible nightmares, experiencing sleep paralysis where I felt as if someone was holding me down and suffocating me.

This happened night after night for two to three months, which made me terrified of falling asleep.

One night, unable to fall asleep, I turned on the television and began watching Joseph Prince's program. He was talking about God's love for me. I wondered, "How can God love me? How do I experience this love?" Praise God, that led me to inviting Jesus into my heart that very night.

Not too long after that, God led me to Pastor Prince's message about the holy anointing oil. My mother and I prayed over the oil and I anointed my door with it. Finally, all my fears of falling asleep at night fled. I experienced rest and felt the love of God so tangibly, it helped me sleep like a baby—that night and thereafter.

Today, I'm a completely different person. I don't smoke, I'm living a joyful life, and know God loves me. I also have compassion toward others and have no desire to be in sinful relationships. People have remarked that I look younger and exude a loving spirit. My family relationships have also been wonderfully restored.

Thank you, Pastor Prince, for preaching the love and Word of God. Through God's grace, I have been delivered from a life of pain and misery. I am now a happy, loving, youthful, and mighty woman of God!

Home Anointed with Oil Protected from Fire

JOAN | WASHINGTON, UNITED STATES

My husband and I have been listening to teachings on the anointing oil by Pastor Joseph Prince. After learning about its significance, we prepared oil that we prayed over and sanctified in small bottles that we carried wherever we went. We also anointed our home with the oil.

One morning, I was awoken by the fire alarm in our apartment building. I smelled smoke the moment I opened the front door. However, I had a sense of peace and knew we were safe. Still, I got my three kids out of the building.

Outside, our neighbor told me that her patio was on fire. After making sure she was all right, we sat in our van watching the firefighters put out the fire. As I sat there watching with my kids, I knew God was telling me that He had protected us. Praise God!

CLOSING WORDS

Beloved, applying the anointing oil, like partaking of the Holy Communion is not just about obtaining your healing or blessing. It's about being conscious of all that our Lord Jesus has done for you and receiving all that He died to give you.

I have shared more on the benefits and truths of the anointing oil in other teaching resources. Here are two suggested ones I hope you will avail yourself to from my ministry website at **JosephPrince.org**:

1.

THE POWER OF THE ANOINTING OIL (2-DVD ALBUM)

2.

EXPERIENCE HEALTH, PROTECTION & PROVISION —THE POWER OF THE HOLY COMMUNION, ANOINTING OIL & TITHING (3-SERMON ALBUM)

You can also find out more about the anointing oil from my ministry website. And if you have been blessed by the testimonies in this booklet, do check out the Praise Reports page for other inspiring stories.

As you begin to make the grain, the wine, and the oil a part of your daily walk as a believer, may you receive and walk in a greater and greater measure of not just healing, but all the blessings that are part of your blood-bought inheritance in Christ!

• • •

Special Appreciation

Special thanks and appreciation to all who have sent in their testimonies and praise reports to us. Kindly note that all testimonies are received in good faith and edited only for brevity and fluency. Names have been changed to protect the writers' privacy.

Salvation Prayer

If you would like to receive all that Jesus has done for you and make Him your Lord and Savior, please pray this prayer:

Lord Jesus, thank You for loving me and dying for me on the cross. Your precious blood washes me clean of every sin. You are my Lord and my Savior, now and forever. I believe You rose from the dead and that You are alive today. Because of Your finished work, I am now a beloved child of God and heaven is my home. Thank You for giving me eternal life and filling my heart with Your peace and joy. Amen.

We Would Like to Hear from You

If you have prayed the salvation prayer or if you have a testimony to share after reading this book, please tell us about it via **JosephPrince.org/praise**. We'd love to hear from you!

Connect with Us

Visit JosephPrince.org today to:

Be Inspired—Sign up for our FREE daily inspirational emails.

Be Encouraged—Read about how the gospel of grace is making a difference one life at a time.

Watch Joseph—Catch his FREE daily broadcast on-demand and receive the gospel of grace anytime, anywhere.

For bite-sized inspirations on-the-go, follow Joseph on:

f fb.com/JosephPrince

@JosephPrince

twitter.com/JosephPrince

Other Books by Joseph Prince

Live the Let-Go Life

Grace Revolution

The Prayer of Protection

The Power of Right Believing

Unmerited Favor

Destined to Reign

The Prayer of Protection Devotional

Glorious Grace

Reign in Life

Destined to Reign Devotional

100 Days of Right Believing

100 Days of Favor

Provision Promises

Healing Promises

For more information on these books and other inspiring resources, visit JosephPrince.org.

My Reflections

....

....

....

....

....

....

....

....

....

....

....

....

....

....

....

....

....

....

....

....

....

....

....

....

"I have come that they may have life,
and that they may have *it* more abundantly."
JOHN 10:10

My Reflections

....

....

....

....

....

....

....

....

....

....

....

....

....

. . . .

. . . .

. . . .

. . . .

. . . .

. . . .

. . . .

. . . .

. . . .

. . . .

. . . .

. . . .

. . . .

And my God shall supply all your need
according to His riches in glory by Christ Jesus.
PHILIPPIANS 4:19